S0-BAO-462

Bobbie and the Play

Monica Hughes
Illustrated by Lisa Smith

Rigby®

A Harcourt Achieve Imprint

www.Rigby.com
1-800-531-5015

Bobbie, Carlos, and Tilly wanted
to be in the school play.

The Ugly Duckling

characters:

☆ One cat.
☆ One dog.
☆ One gray duckling.
☆ Two white swans.
☆ Six yellow ducklings.

Mrs. Walksfar said,
"Tilly, you can be the cat.
Carlos, you can be the dog,
and, Bobbie, you can be the gray duckling."

4

Bobbie didn't want to be the gray duckling.

In the play, the gray duckling went
to see the yellow ducklings.
The yellow ducklings said, "You are ugly.
Go away and don't come back."
The gray duckling was sad.

Then the gray duckling went
to see the cat.
The cat said, "You are ugly.
Go away and don't come back."
The gray duckling was very sad.

Then the gray duckling went
to see the dog.
The dog said, "You are ugly.
Go away and don't come back."
The gray duckling was **very** sad.

"I don't like being the gray duckling," said Bobbie.

"Don't be sad," said Mrs. Walksfar.
"The gray duckling becomes a swan now!"

"Wow!" said the white swans.
"The gray duckling became a swan!"

Bobbie **loved** being the swan.